Crawley Bugs

Dave Crawley

ANIMALHERO® ANIMALHERO®KIDS
Loving Life with Animals®

AnimalHero®
AnimalHero® **Kids**
AnimalHero® **Family**

Welcome to our global conversation about animals and their people.

We connect AnimalHero friends and AnimalHeroKids across six continents.

We inspire and educate children and adults to be kind stewards of animals, while promoting the joy of reading, writing, and creativity.

AnimalHero.com
AnimalHeroKids.com

Facebook.com/TheAnimalHero
Facebook.com/TheAnimalHeroKids

Crawley Bugs

Don't worry, these rhymes don't bite.

Dave Crawley

ANIMALHERO® ANIMALHERO®KIDS
Loving Life with Animals®

Crawley Bugs

© 2013 Dave Crawley, Pet Laureate for AnimalHero® Kids

AnimalHero.com
AnimalHeroKids.com
AnimalHero® Productions
AnimalHero® Books
Established 2005
Laurel Herman, Founder
Dave Crawley, Pet Laureate

Laurel Herman, Producer/Creative Director, Designer
John Tollett, Digital Typographic Illustration, Production

laurel@animalhero.com
dave@animalhero.com

© 2005, *How To Write A Silly Poem,* page 48

Printed and bound in the United States of America
10 9 8 7 6 5 4 3 2

Dedication

For Laurel, who gently removes wayward bugs from the house,
and carefully places them in the yard.
Even though she's sometimes squeamish.
Thank you for making this book possible.

Welcome!

Kids are fascinated with bugs. We are too. Bugs that fly! Bugs that swim!

Web spinning spiders, and delicate insects on flowers. Beautiful butterflies. Beetles that dart about in ponds. Funny looking bugs. (Ever wonder if bugs think *we're* funny looking?)

These pages are filled with "word pictures" describing tiny creatures that outnumber all other species combined. We are also fascinated by the alphabet, and the fact that our entire world can be described with just 26 letters.

As we read, we make pictures in our minds. Sometimes, our imaginary pictures take the form of the very words we're reading. Playing with the alphabet helps us all become better readers and writers.

When we visit schools for *AnimalHero®Kids Workshops and Classes,* we're inspired by the creativity of students. Young writers read aloud, write stories and poems, make artwork, improvise dramas, and share ideas that spring from their imaginations.

In *Crawley Bugs,* with John Tollett's help, we had visual fun with words from the poems.

Now it's your turn! We invite you to color these pages. Grab markers, crayons, and pencils. Feel free to make this book your creative playground and sketchbook. Write! Draw! Doodle! Play! Have fun!

Would you like to share your creativity? If you wish, email JPEGs of your bug drawings and poems to dave@animalhero.com, and we may post your drawings on the Internet for other AnimalHero®Kids and AnimalHero®Friends to enjoy.

Celebrate the wondrous world of words. And, of course, bugs!

Dave Crawley *Author*

Laurel Herman *Designer*

CONTENTS

A Cricket in the Thicket.............9

Legs................................10

Time to Prey........................11

Bugged About Names................12

Lovely Ladybug.....................13

Angela Tarantula...................14

Black Widow........................15

Whirligig..........................16

Water Strider......................17

Metamorphosis......................18

Monarch............................19

Fritillary Frolic....................20

Click!..............................21

Antlion............................22

The Silverfish is Not a Fish.........23

Stink!..............................24

Grasshopper Juice..................25

A Spider Drops In..................26

Red Spotted Purple.................27

House Party.........................28

Locust Lunch.......................29

He-Bug, She-Bug....................30

Velvet?.............................31

The Miserable Mosquito...........32

Walking Stick......................33

Ambush!............................34

Pill Bug...........................35

June Bug...........................36

Cicada.............................37

Longlegs...........................38

Woolly Bear........................39

Dance of the Damselfly.............40

Flicker.............................41

Song of the Katydid................42

Busy Beetle........................43

How Long?..........................44

One Day............................45

How To Write A Silly Poem............48

BUZZING BUSY BUZZING BUSY BUZZING BUSY BUZ

Did you ever listen to the sounds of an overgrown field on a hot summer day? The chirping of crickets? The buzzing of noisy cicadas? But watch out for the quiet one...

A Cricket in the Thicket

There's a cricket in the thicket.
I can hear him "skritchy-skree!"
I can hear the busy buzzing
of a fuzzy-buzzy bee.
In the shade a big cicada
goes "ka-chicka-chicka-chinner,"
as a hungry humming housefly
makes a bee-line for my dinner.
But the spider is a hider
in a corner of the wall.
She spins a nest for noisy guests,
and
      makes
          no
             sound
                at
                  all.

I CAN HEAR THE BUSY BUZZING OF A FUZZY-BUZZY BEE

No wonder he can

scoot

so fast

Legs

How many legs does a bug have? That depends on whether it's an insect or a spider. Or a bug with too many legs to count.

The insect has six tiny legs.
The spider walks on eight.
They crawl on walls with sticky feet,
which help them elevate.

What bug could match the centipede?
A hundred legs, or more!
No wonder he can scoot so fast
across the cellar floor!

That sounds like fun, but when it's time
for me to tie my shoe,
I wouldn't want a hundred feet.
I'm glad I just have two.

The praying mantis is a large green or brown insect, with long front legs. The way those legs are bent makes it appear that she is praying. Or perhaps we should say "preying."

Time to Prey

The praying mantis prays for prey –
for bumbling bugs to pass her way.
And when they face her mighty snare,
the prey she prayed for has no prayer.

her mighty snare

I never saw a dragon *fly*

- You may have
- worn a yellow
- jacket. But have
- you ever seen a
- dragon fly?
- Yet, dragonflies
- are everywhere.
- And don't get
- me started on
- earwigs.

Bugged About Names

I never saw a dragon fly,
except in Fairy Tales.
I never met a woolly bear,
while walking wooded trails.

I wouldn't wear an ear wig.
(I've never even tried.)
And if I see a house fly,
I hope I'm not inside.

A walking stick might do the trick
while hiking down the coast.
If ever I see butter fly,
I hope it lands on toast.

I don't wear a yellow jacket,
or eat a honey bee.
But if my dog begins to scratch,
I know it's time to "flea."

Most of us have seen tiny round and spotted beetles known as ladybugs. They eat even smaller insects called aphids. And that's a good thing.

Lovely Ladybug

We love the lovely ladybug,
decked out in red and black.
Each fall, the lady vanishes.
Each summer, she comes back

And while she's here, she dines on pests
that eat our favorite plants.
When tiny aphids pass her way,
those bugs don't stand a chance.

We love the lovely ladybug,
so delicate and small,
because the lady loves the bugs
that we don't like at all.

we love
the lovely
ladybug

just in case, I'll give her space
SPACE

The tarantula is the largest spider in the world. Her bite is not likely to make you sick. But it does hurt.

Angela Tarantula

Angela Tarantula
is fearsome to behold.
Face so scary. Legs so hairy.
Eyes so dark and cold.

She prowls at night. A frightful sight.
A shadow in the dark.
And then she'll spring, with fangs that sting.
Her venom finds its mark.

To pass her way, by night or day,
is reason for alarm.
Despite the fright, her painful bite
won't cause us lasting harm.

But just in case, I'll give her space,
and if she will agree,
Angela Tarantula
can stay away from me.

The black widow
is a shiny black
spider with red or
orange markings
on her belly.
She's not as big
or scary looking
as the tarantula.
But her bite
is much more
poisonous.
She is almost
always alone.
There's a reason
for that.

Black Widow

Don't feel sorry for this widow,
though she's always on her own.
When guests arrive, she eats them
(which explains why she's alone).

She will always be a widow,
since she even eats her mate.
She has a reputation
as a most unpleasant date.

She's the queen of deadly spiders,
on a solitary throne.
Don't feel sorry for this widow.
It's her taste to be alone.

on a solitary

THRONE

Delighting in Diving

Does any insect have as much fun as the whirligig? The little black beetle zips back and forth across the glassy surface of a pond, then dives under the water, only to pop to the surface somewhere else.

Whirligig

The whirligig beetle darts hither and fro.
You never can guess where this beetle will go.
Zipping and flipping and jigging and jagging,
the whirligig zigs when you thought he'd be zagging.

Skimming the surface of puddles and ponds,
he darts in the shadows of cattail fronds.
Delighting in diving, and dancing about —
a fun loving fellow, without any doubt.

But if you try whirling like whirligigs whirl,
you'll get a surprise as you spin and you twirl.
You'll get a bit dizzy before you get through it.
Leave whirling to beetles who know how to do it.

Water striders are insects with very thin legs. They seem to skate across the surface of a lake or a pond. The only parts that touch the water are the tips of their tiny feet.

Water Strider

The strider is a glider
on the surface of a lake.
Zipping. Slidey-slipping.
Leaving ripples in his wake.

A fascinating skater.
Yet there's one thing I don't get:
He spends his life in water,
without ever getting wet.

fascinating

Skater

Wings
he'll spread his

Metamorphosis

The ugly caterpillar
has skin that's much too tight.
With stubby legs and body,
he's not a pretty sight.

But like the ugly duckling,
his best days lie ahead—
emerging from his chrysallis
with wings of blue and red.

Like the swan, he'll spread his wings,
and sail above us all—
looking down on leafy plants
where caterpillars crawl.

If you don't like the way you look,
try not to be so glum.
It's less important who you are
than who you might become.

Most caterpillars are not very attractive. But after he's eaten enough to get nice and fat, the caterpillar spins a chrysalis, and sort of hibernates for a while. During this time, he's changing into a butterfly. This amazing transformation is called "metamorphosis."

Your kingdom spans two thousand miles

The monarch is one of the most beautiful and amazing insects of all. The familiar orange butterfly with thin black stripes lives throughout North America. When the weather turns cold, the monarch migrates hundreds of miles, to a winter home in Mexico. He and other monarchs sleep in the branches of trees, and wait for Sping.

Monarch

You're the monarch of the butterflies.
The undisputed king.
Your kingdom spans two thousand miles.
You pass this way each spring.

From Mexico to Monterey.
From Florida to Maine.
You soar aloft on royal wings,
through wind and icy rain.

You migrate, just as eagles do.
And when your flight is done,
you flutter down to share with us
a season in the sun.

When Autumn comes, you'll bid farewell,
and once again take wing –
for butterflies in distant lands
are waiting for their king.

You pass this way each Spring

frittering
and other silly things

Fritillary butterflies come in different colors. Most of them have orange wings, with a mix of dark designs and spots. You're likely to see them fluttering around in meadows and woodlands. They seem to be having a lot of fun.

Fritillary Frolic

The merry little fritillary
has a lot of fun.
Every stop is temporary,
till the day is done.

Then the little fritillary
rests his weary wings.
Tomorrow's meant for frittering
and other silly things.

Did you ever lie on your back, and wish you could just pop to your feet, without having to pull yourself up? A long, grey insect called the click beetle can do just that! If you listen closely, you can even hear the "click."

Click!

Click! goes the click beetle, back to his feet.
He's the funniest beetle you're likely to meet.

Whenever he stumbles and lands on his back,
a quick little "click" and he's on the right track.

I wish I could click like click beetles click.
To flip in mid-air is a marvelous trick.

The key is to click in a very small space.
Try clicking too far, and you'll fall on your face.

I wish I could do it. I'd really be slick,
if I only could click like click beetles click.

I wish I could click like click beetles click

The antlion is as scary as he sounds, if you happen to be an ant. He digs a cone-shaped pit in the sand, then hides beneath the sand at the bottom. When an ant or other insect stumbles in, the antlion pops out and grabs him in his great big jaws. Say goodbye to the ant.

Antlion

The antlion hides in his shadowy lair,
and hopes to catch stumbling bugs in his snare.
He digs out a hole with a slippery slope.
Ants that slide in must abandon all hope,

Just one inch across, it's a very small pit.
But, for his purpose, it's just the right fit.
This lion won't roar in the dark of the night.
But if you're an ant, beware of his bite.

THIS LION WON'T ROAR

SLIPPY ❖ SLIDEY ❖ SLIPPY ❖ SLIDEY ❖ SLIPPY ❖ SLIDEY
SLIDEY ♣ SLIPPY ♣ SLIDEY ❖ SLIPPY ❖ SLIDEY ❖ SLIPPY ❖ SLIDEY
SLIPPY ✳ SLIDEY ✳ SLIPPY ✳ SLIDEY ✳ SLIPPY ✳ SLIDEY ✳ SLIPPEY ✳
SLIDEY ◆ SLIPPY ◆ SLIDEY ◆ SLIPPY ◆ SLIDEY ✳ SLIPPY ✳ SLIDEY ✳
SLIPPY ❖ SLIDEY ❖ SLIPPY ◆ SLIPPY ◆ SLIDEY ◆ SLIPPEY ◆
SLIPPY ✳ SLIDEY ✳ SLIPPY ❖ SLIDEY ❖ SLIPPY ❖ SLIDEY ❖
SLIDEY ✳ SLIPPY ✳ SLIDEY

He's grey and scaley,
like a fish. He likes
damp places, like a fish.
When he runs across
the floor, his body
wiggles back and forth
just like… well, a fish.
In fact, he's called a
silverfish. But he is not
a fish. He's an insect.

The Silverfish is Not a Fish

The slippy slidey silverfish
is not a fish at all.
A fish does not have legs to run,
and climb the bathroom wall.

Although the silverfish has scales,
as other fishes do,
no fish would eat the things he eats –
like crumpled leaves and glue.

His ancestors go back in time,
before the dinosaur.
Yet somehow he survived to run
across my kitchen floor.

No other fish could hide in cracks,
or scurry down the hall.
But as I said, the silverfish
is not a fish at all.

Have you ever seen a stink bug in your house? They usually drop by in the winter, to get out of the cold. When they're disturbed, their scent glands give off a stinky smell. Could that odor also be caused by the smelly places they move into when spring arrives?

Stink!

The little brown stink bug
lives down by the stream.
He suffers, I'm certain,
from low self-esteem.

Avoided by others
he sluggishly slinks.
There's no way around it:
the little guy stinks.

His dinner is larvae.
He has no dessert.
Then he crawls under leaves
and sleeps in the dirt.

In winter, when weather
turns bitterly cold,
he may enter your house,
still smelling of mold.

So pity the stink bug.
For this much is true:
If you lived where he did,
then you would stink, too.

Grasshoppers don't chew tobacco

Have you ever picked up a grasshopper, only to have him spit gooey brown liquid onto your fingers? It's often called tobacco juice because of the way it looks. Although it really isn't, it's unpleasant enough to make birds and other predators let him go. It also works on humans.

Grasshopper Juice

Grasshoppers don't chew tobacco,
although it may seem that they do.
The juice that they spit on your fingers
is just a small puddle of goo.

It's actually sort of disgusting.
It's sticky and icky and wet.
He spits as a form of protection,
whenever he's faced with a threat.

Tobacco juice (that's what we call it,
because it's so gummy and brown)
is the grasshopper's manner of saying,
"It's best if you just put me down."

Imagine you're having lunch.
Maybe you're looking at that spinach on your plate.
And at that moment...

A spider dropped onto my spinach

A Spider Drops In

A spider dropped onto my spinach,
and though I was happy to share,
all she was doing
was simply pursuing
the fly that was already there.

The butterfly known as the
red spotted purple has purple wings,
with red spots at the tips.

WHAT MORE NEED BE SAID?

Red Spotted Purple

The red spotted purple
is purple and red.
He also is spotted.
What more need be said?

Nobody wants termites in the house. That's because they eat the wood that holds your house together. And the wood boring beetle lays eggs that turn into worms, which also eat wood. And they're not the only ones.

House Party

The wood boring beetle worm loves to eat wood.
His neighbor, the termite, thinks timbers taste good.
The same could be said for the wood-eating louse.
Their plan for a picnic was eating my house.

Concealed in my walls, they were happy to munch.
My counters and cupboards were perfect for lunch.
They came back for dinner, and chewed on my floors.
And then, for dessert, they devoured my doors.

Those gluttonous wood-chomping bugs are now gone.
My house in their bellies, they simply moved on.
I have been forced to move into a tent.
The worst part of all is they never paid rent.

happy to munch

His manners are frightful

No farmer wants to see a swarm of locusts attacking his crops. These greedy grasshoppers eat a tremendous amount of food, considering their size.

Locust Lunch

The locust is greedy, an eating machine.
His manners are frightful. You'll see what I mean.
Without using napkins, or even a plate,
this glutton will gobble ten times his own weight!

He grazes on grasses, while swallowing weeds,
till all are devoured. Yes, even the seeds!
If you ate as much as a locust can munch,
you'd end up consuming the world's biggest lunch.

Like forty-eight carrots. A bucket of beans.
Twenty-two turkeys and sixty sardines.
Seventy steaks. Six pounds of soufflé.
That would be LESS than he eats in a day!

The locust is focused on nothing but food.
He stays until all of the crops have been chewed.
We only can hope, as he comes for his feeding,
another bug eats him before he starts eating.

"SHOULD WE CALL HER Mommy Longlegs?"

Is a daddy longlegs always a daddy? Is a ladybug always a lady? Not always!

He-Bug, She-Bug

Should we call her "Mommy Longlegs"
if the "Daddy" is a "she?"
Would the sowbug be a "boarbug"
when the sowbug is a "he?"

If ladybugs and damselflies
should happen to be male,
and katydids aren't "ladydids,"
should different names prevail?

It's hard to know what kind of bug
the bug you see may be,
when the "he-bug" is a "she-bug"
and the "she-bug" is a "he."

The velvet ant is not really velvet. In fact, she's not even an ant. Although the female has no wings, and looks like a great big fuzzy ant, she's really a wasp. She also stings like a wasp!

Velvet?

Soft as velvet, velvet ant.
Dressed in colors that enchant.
Would you give a happy purr
if I stroke your velvet fur?

Could I touch your coat of red?
May I scratch your fuzzy head?
Cold, dark eyes say "Do not dare,"
warning me of danger there.

Even though you creep and crawl,
you are not an ant, at all.
"Velvet wasp" is more precise.
Those who touch will pay the price.

Soft as velvet, velvet ant.
I would pet you, but I can't.
Though your colors may delight,
you don't have a velvet bite.

DRESSED IN COLORS THAT enchant

The Miserable Mosquito

The miserable mosquito
was hatched within a swamp—
a slimy grimy mudhole,
where alligators stomp.

Though born a wiggly wriggler,
she quickly learned to fly.
She looked for folks to feed on
(a plentiful supply).

And now, she's found my bedroom.
She's whining in the dark.
I'm swinging and I'm swatting,
but always miss the mark

For the miserable mosquito,
it's just a playful romp.
I wish the gators got her
in the slimy, grimy swamp.

Is any insect more despised than the mosquito? She lays her eggs in still water, ranging from puddles to ponds. Or, in this case, a slimy, grimy swamp.

Swatting Swinging Swat

walking through the wood

The walking stick appears to be just that: a walking stick. This insect, shaped like a twig, might be seen rocking up and down in the branch of a tree. He might be seen walking slowly though a thicket. But most of the time, he can't seen at all.

Walking Stick

I thought I saw a walking stick.
It surely was a shocking stick.
A scrawny, awkward stalking stick
a-walking through the wood.

Too quiet for a talking stick,
he'll never be a squawking stick.
He simply was a walking stick.
Then silently, he stood.

As I approached the walking stick—
a momentary balking stick—
he then became a rocking stick
and clambered up a tree.

He watched me like a gawking stick.
Since branches hid the mocking stick,
I couldn't see the walking stick.
But I know he saw me.

If you were an insect (and it's a good thing you're not) you'd have to always check to see if the ambush bug is sneaking up on you. But there are times when this sneaky insect should do some checking of his own.

Ambush!

The ambush bug hides
in flowers and plants,
just waiting to spring
on slow moving ants.

But any stray bug
is certain to please.
The ambush bug even
eats spiders and bees!

He stares at his prey,
prepared to attack,
while failing to see
the mantis in back.

Clamped in her claws,
he cannot get free.
The "ambusher" now
is the "ambushee."

If you want to hide
so no one can find you,
always be certain
there's no one behind you.

waiting

You'll **never** hear pill bugs complaining

If you've ever lifted a rock to see what's underneath, there's a good chance you saw some oval shaped bugs that curl into a ball to protect themselves. They don't have bright colors. They can't fly. They just like living in the dark.

Pill Bug

The little old pill bug is gloomy and grey.
He rarely goes out for a walk.
If you approach him, he'll scurry away,
to his hiding place under a rock.

Lift up the rock and he'll curl in a ball.
He looks like a little grey stone.
He tries to pretend that he's not there at all,
and hopes that you'll leave him alone.

He's very content to live life in the dark.
You'll never hear pill bugs complaining.
He amuses himself by chewing on bark.
(For a pill bug, that's fine entertaining.)

And that's about it. What more can we say?
His life doesn't need much exploring.
Let's do him a favor, and just walk away.
The pill bug can't help that he's boring.

Rattles AND CLATTERS AND THRASHING AND CRASHING

June Bug

June bugs are large, clumsy insects that show up in late spring. They're attracted to light. You may hear them bouncing off your windows on warm nights in June.

The June bug appears between April and June.
That's when he exits his winter cocoon.
This bumbling beetle, attracted by light,
then rattles and clatters your shutters at night.

And when he's not thrashing and crashing about
(a sound which, perhaps, we could all do without),
this ravenous insect is spending his hours
consuming our crops, and feeding on flowers.

Then, for dessert, he may chew on your lawn.
Do not despair, for he soon will be gone.
When the calendar changes, he'll no longer fly.
The bug named for June will be gone by July.

Cicada

Seventeen years the cicada has slept
(a nap that I find very hard to accept).
Seventeen years he prepared for this squall.
Cicada's awake, and I can't sleep at all.

Chitter
Chatter Chitter
Chitter Chatter
Chitter Chatter
Chatter

Cicadas spend the first years

of their lIves, up to seventeen years,

living quietly underground.

But when they finally emerge for a summer in the sun,

they make up for lost time by creating a racket that

no other insect can match.

A gentle touch

As you can guess from his name, Daddy Longlegs has long legs. Eight long legs in fact, though he's only a distant relative of the spider. The legs are very thin, and very delicate.

Longlegs

Daddy longlegs doesn't have strong legs.
Sad to say, they're fragile.
When one is lost, there is a cost:
he isn't very agile.

A gentle touch is all it takes
to lose a leg or two.
So do not bother Daddy, please,
and he won't bother you.

It's best to let him go his way,
and leave him to his fate.
Though he'd get by on seven legs,
he's better off on eight.

is all it takes

What's the weather woolly bear?

A caterpillar known as the woolly bear is often spotted on wooded trails in the late days of autumn. Though he will eventually emerge from his cocoon as a tiger moth, at the moment he's a fuzzy little creature with black coloring in the front and back, and a thick orange band in the middle. Some say the width of that band tells us how cold the winter will be. That's not really true. But it makes a good story.

Woolly Bear

Fuzzy-wuzzy woolly bear,
covered up with so much hair.
You must know that winter's near.
Coming closer. Almost here.

What's the weather, woolly bear?
Will I need long underwear?
Caterpillar that you are,
can you really see that far?

Autumn leaves begin to glow.
Chilly breezes start to blow.
As we near the harvest moon,
spin yourself a warm cocoon.

Soon you'll sleep, alone and still.
Winter comes. The air grows chill.
Now I'm dressing just like you.
I feel fuzzy-wuzzy, too.

delightfully sprightful and fun

If you visit a pond on a sunny day, you may see a long, thin insect with green, blue, red or yellow wings that shimmer as she flitters about. This is the dance of the damselfly.

Dance of the Damselfly

The dance of the delicate damselfly
is delightfully sprightful and fun -
cavorting in cattails down by the pond,
in the glimmery glow of the sun.

With bobbing blue body and shimmery wings,
this damsel is truly inspired.
Dancing on air, her wings do the work.
Her feet will never get tired.

I love watching fireflies blinking on warm summer nights. One night, I decided to catch one and put him in a jar. But it wasn't long before I changed my mind.

Flicker

Fireflies flicker and flutter in flight.
Gleaming white beacons that flash in the night.
One has just landed. But he won't get far.
I'll sneak up and – gotcha! He's trapped in my jar.

But now it appears that the beacon I caught
is not lighting up quite as much as I thought.
He's losing his glimmer, without any doubt.
His light has grown dimmer, and soon may go out.

I still have a chance to undo what I did.
Quietly, gently, I unscrew the lid.
He pauses a moment, then quickly takes flight.
There! in the distance! He's flashing his light.

I'd like to imagine he's blinking for me.
The light that shines best is the light that is free.

The light that shines best is the light that is free

He looks like a grasshopper, except he's bigger. And greener. In spite of the lovely name "Katy," this insect is named for the male of the species. He makes a sound like, "Katy did, Katy didn't!" over and over again, hoping to attract females. It almost always works.

talented Singer

Song of the Katydid

"Katy did! Katy didn't!"
The katydid sings.
He then flies away,
on wafer-thin wings.

He's a talented singer
in emerald green —
the handsomest hopper
that ever was seen.

Though others may fly
much farther than he,
his music is matchless.
He's never off-key.

While chattering cousins
may clatter and buzz,
no bug ever sang
like the katydid does.

Sometimes bugs just get lost. They wind up some place they dodn't really want to be. That's how it was with a busy little beetle that I found in the house.

Crawl into my hand, AND I'LL GIVE YOU a Ride

Busy Beetle

Hey, busy beetle,
don't roam on my rug!
A rug is no place
for a wandering bug.

Crawl into my hand,
and I'll give you a ride.
There! Do the rest
of your roaming outside.

Have you ever tried to see how long it takes for a bee to flap its wings? It can't be done. Those wings flap faster than the eye can see.

How Long?

How long does it take
till a second is done?
Enough time to count
"One thousand and one?"

It's just long enough,
as the clock tower chimes
for the wings of a bee
to flap two hundred times.

the wings of a bee

One Day

Mayfly! One-day fly!
One-day-in-May fly!
What are your plans,
one-day-to-play fly?

Millions of Mayflies,
hatching at dawn,
flutter in flower beds,
dance on the lawn.

Fresh wings of freedom.
But you must make haste.
Hours are fleeting.
There's no time to waste

No time to wander,
to dawdle or dream.
Eggs must be laid
in the rippling stream.

The stream where you lived
a year, as you grew,
awaiting your time
to start life anew.

One day. That is all.
Your job is soon done.
Now rest, in the dwindling
glow of the sun.

Though your brief moment
is melting away,
you've made the most
of a mighty fine day.

IMAGINE

that you had
one day—
just one day—
to bask in the
sunshine.
To fly like a bird.
That's all the
Mayfly has.
This insect's larva
spends a year
growing, waiting,
in the mud
and pebbles at
the bottom of
a stream.
At last,
he rises up
to see the
world for
one glorius day
in the month
of May.

a mighty fine day

Dave Crawley

is an award winning TV reporter and celebrated children's author. He has taped more than 4,000 human interest stories for KDKA-TV (CBS) and WQED-TV (PBS) in Pittsburgh, Pennsylvania. Awards include 13 Mid-Atlantic EMMYS and an Edward R. Murrow Award for broadcast news writing.

Known for his rhyming stories on KDKA, Dave branched out into children's literature. His first book, the critically-acclaimed *Cat Poems,* honors our feline friends. His second book, *Dog Poems,* was selected as one of "The Best Children's Books of the Year" by the Bank Street Children's Book Committee. Dave's book of school poems, *Reading, Rhyming, and 'Rithmetic,* received a starred review ("Highly Recommended") from the Library Media Connection. All were published by Boyds Mills Press (Wordsong).

Dave also has numerous poems in nine anthologies, including *I Invited a Dragon to Dinner* (Philomel Books). He has published dozens of poems in 13 national children's magazines, including "Ranger Rick," "Cricket," and "Jack and Jill."

Laurel Herman

is a creative director, photographer and writer. She has an M.A. in Art Therapy, specializing in working with children and adolescents. Her master's thesis focused on developing empathy in children, as it relates to the human-animal bond.

Laurel founded AnimalHero® and AnimalHero®Kids in 2005, during a visit to India. She met three young girls who took extraordinary measures to care for homeless animals.

The girls asked Laurel to help spread the word that kindness to animals is important. Laurel promised she would establish an international organization to connect and celebrate children and adults who help animals. *Promise kept.*

AnimalHero®Kids
Workshops and Classes at Schools

Dave Crawley, AnimalHero Pet Laureate
Laurel Herman, AnimalHero Founder

Dave and Laurel give AnimalHero®Kids Workshops and Classes at schools, where students are inspired to be kind stewards of animals while having fun with reading, writing and creativity.

Students are active participants, reading Dave's poems aloud, becoming empowered to write their own. Classes talk about their experiences with animals. Kids love to perform dramas from Dave's story poems, and help him create "Construct-a Poems" on the spot.

Be part of our AnimalHero community! Listen to podcasts and audio selections from select 2010 AnimalHero workshops. Visit us on Facebook and connect with AnimalHero® friends around the world.

AnimalHero.com
AnimalHeroKids.com
Facebook.com/TheAnimalHero
Facebook.com/TheAnimalHeroKids
iTunes: AnimalHero

How To Write A Silly Poem

R is for "Rhyme," and most poems do.
When writing such poems, the rhyme should be true.
"Ride," "glide," and "pride" don't quite rhyme with "fright."
When you write a rhyme, make sure it sounds right.

H is for "Humor." "Hilarious," too
(like that little old lady who lived in a shoe).
You can use silly words in this kind of spoof—
like "albatross," "blunderbuss," "bombast" and "goof."

Y is for "You." Without any doubt,
you are the person you know most about.
When writing a poem, the best way to go
is to write about things that you already know.

M is for "Meter," the rhythm you choose.
Remember, no matter what meter you use,
it's easy to tell if the meter is wrong:
If lines are too short,
or else they just seem to go on and on and on and end up much too long.

E is for "Edit." That means to go back,
and see if your poem is on the right track.
Some lines may work fine, while others just won't.
Keep what you like, and erase what you don't

S for "Surprise," at the end of your rhyme.
A twist, unexpected, will work every time.
If your ending is clever, amusing and fun,
you can relax, for your poem is done!

Write Draw Doodle Play

Write Draw Doodle Play

Write Draw *Doodle* Play

Write Draw Doodle Play

Write Draw Doodle Play

Write Draw Doodle Play

Made in the USA
Middletown, DE
04 October 2020